Burnt Island

Burnt Island

Three Suites

D. Nurkse

Alfred A. Knopf   *New York*   *2005*

THIS IS A BORZOI BOOK
PUBLISHED BY ALFRED A. KNOPF

www.aaknopf.com

Knopf, Borzoi Books, and the colophon are registered trademarks
of
Random House, Inc.

Owing to limitations of space, all acknowledgments to print pre-
viously published material may be found at the end of the book.

Library of Congress Cataloging-in-Publication Data
Nurkse, D., [date]
Burnt Island : three suites / D. Nurkse.—1st ed.
p.   cm.
ISBN 1-4000-4350-6
1. City and town life—Poetry.   2. Marine animals—Poetry.
3. Islands—Poetry.   4. Nature—Poetry.   I. Title.

PS3564.U76B87 2005
811'.54—dc22   2004048812

Manufactured in the United States of America
First Edition

For Beth, with love

I slept not since the Conquest.

  —*"Tom O'Bedlam"*

I see the ocean of love
but not the raft on which to cross it.

  —*Tiruvalluvar*

. . . we came to perceive life as a force as tangible
as the physical realities of the sea . . .

  —*Rachel Carson*

Contents

Defenses of the Ocean

The
Reunification
Center

My Father's Closet

1 HAT

As soon as I put it on
Brooklyn went dark,
but when I took it off
my wooden horse stared at me
with dazzling glass eyes.

2 COAT

The shirred hem
swished on the floor.
Huge shoulders sloped
like pines under snow.
A panel in the lapel
read: *Kuut, Tallinn*
in thread letters.
I hid at the center
behind jet buttons
too round to undo.
That coarse-nap wool
outlasted Estonian winter
but now the moths
left a trellis of holes
so it was never dark
when I curled up
hugging my knees.
My mother cried out:

Who are you? I answered
in my deepest voice:
His coat.

3 SHOES

I shoved my hands in
and taught them to walk:
now stumble: now march
against your will, left, right,
to the Narva Front:

now dance:
                          and somewhere
in that immense city
where snow trembled
in high lit windows,
a footstep receded,
rapid, urgent,
indelible as a name.

Night Flight

I made friends
with a dead sparrow
I found on the sidewalk,
rigid in the center
of a carved heart.
I groomed it scrupulously.
The only blood
was a fleck in the eye.
I could make the sleek wings
glide and twirl
despite a force
that held them shut.
As we were soaring
among those trees
scored with dates
my mother called.

No, no,
it isn't me,
that breathless name
filling with rage,
then fear, then loneliness.

Saint Luke

1

My mother died and the line
on the monitor went straight.

She who once held me
gently held me tightly
and the orderly coughed
behind a screen.

I brushed a hair from her forehead
and went to the restroom.

When I came back, the orderly
tendered a pile of forms:
sign here—sign here—

2

After nine days of coma
he had wheeled her to a room
with a broken window;
each time I complained
he looked puzzled and said
if you like, I'll fetch a blanket
but I never saw it

3

so now I imagine it—
static-charged, regal, deep-napped—

now I too live in the other world
of cups too light to shatter,
pink knives that can't open skin,
boiled sheets, constant snow
flickering beyond the blind

as if we never lived,
erasing our footprints and the tracks
of the car that brought us
before dawn to a stranger's house.

A Puzzle at Saint Luke

The sky is the hard part:
no landmark, just the contour
of the next piece,

and does it help that the old man
with the tremor is so shy
he just waits, and waiting suits him,

and it's still snowing
in a high oblique window,
so that the light also trembles?

We want to finish the Ascension
so we can be released
and wake in our own beds—

we who are almost whole,
almost ourselves, almost foreign
to these absurd back-slit gowns:

and now his lips shake,
framing a word, always the same,
as if that gap were home.

Two Nights in the Men's Shelter

1

I was the one who never fought
but I was the pilot.
I took nothing and sat awake
while Chickie and LoSurdo dropped acid
and hallucinated their way back
from Subic Bay to Da Nang
in the unworldly beauty
of tracer fire. Sometimes
they shook me gently:
please don't: you mustn't sleep
while we are still in danger
at Khe Sanh. I nodded
and forced myself not to count
raindrops on the tin roof:
again the tug at my sleeve
and the pleading whisper:
don't leave us here
so far behind enemy lines
with just a day's food,
a flashlight and a mirror,
a knife and the four coordinates,
no flares, and the forest
more than ever full of voices.

2

Before dawn Nixon came to me
shattered by alcohol, begging forgiveness
for bombing the Plain of Jars.
I raised two fingers and blessed him.
He left a free man and I woke
in this huge room, interminable rain,
unwavering lamps, the other sleepers
twisting in their separate dreams.

4:00 A.M.

Because it happened
it didn't seem real:
one man beating another.

Maybe after long circling
he'd gained a slight edge
and now he was master,
methodical, limited,
perhaps already wondering
how to stop . . .

the other covered his eyes
any way he could.

We were strolling home
from that miraculous dance
we entered as strangers—
separated by agonized love
we'd bargained our way
down to whispered jokes
about the imploring music
and tight-clinging masks.

We were kinder
than the raised fist
so long as we stood our ground
on K Street, corner of Vine,

still holding hands, coughing
once, twice, you, me,

so he might sense
he was watched and at least
move away from the glare
of those high stooping lamps
about to fade at dawn.

A Walk in Giovanna's Park

Under the immense elm
the children are no bigger than children.

How can anything live
with the heart carved in it so deeply?

The old couple eating saltines
look like twins in the half-light.

A firefly sails past,
the first since we met.

I pull a gold thread
unraveling from your sleeve.

We step carefully here.
The glowworms have begun to flash,

beckoning us to a kingdom
our arrival will destroy.

Don't you know that lovers
like to imagine eternity

while a sparrow pecks at candy wrappers,
staring sideways fiercely?

Lovers have to rest from each other
but there's nowhere in the world.

Even the grass is singed.
Even for the fat white ducks

with painfully orange feet
it's so complicated

to be given a crumb.
Under the immense elm

children are playing with darkness
as if it were clay,

and they've made two small gods
who cannot leave each other.

The Ring

In May when the winged seeds
skitter on the pavement
and pollen clouds the names
carved in the elms,

in a zone of sweatshops,
pawnshops, tenements
with chipped marble stoops,
storefront churches
with penciled signs:
He Who Drinks the Living Water
Shall Never Thirst Again,

in a little hotel
just before the war
and long before dawn:

remember how a kitten
mewed down the corridor
to scratch at our door?

A blue moth beat wildly
in our clouded night glass.

We found a bent playing card
in the twisted sheets,
and a paste-diamond ring.

Remember how we washed
at the porcelain sink,

combing with our fingers,
facing each other naked
in that room with no mirror?

We had no idea how to go on
without the armor of suffering.

The kitten rubbed between us
in a calm frenzy—you, I, I, you—
just born, already famished
for this world, this body.

The Last Judgment

Remember when there were old men
with flowing hair and robes
cinched with frayed string
who toted towering signs
proclaiming the end of the world?
Remember the organ grinders
with bored monkeys? Remember how we met
lovesick and terrified
outside the pawnshop
and then walked side by side,
hands barely touching,
to the Valencia Hotel
to undress each other
by the dazzling flinch
of the neon sign
so that everything happened
in mirror writing?
When we finished
we heard the voices
boring on relentlessly
as if sworn to repeat themselves
at any cost, *Repent, Repent,*

while we dried ourselves
at the sink where a copper stain
glittered below the leaky tap.
And no one returned.
Not you, not I,
not even the stray dog
that followed our ghosts
warily, for a block or two,
then at Dyer Avenue
sat down and scratched,
blinking hopefully, sniffing the dust.

The Evacuation Corridor

1

When I strolled up from the subway
it was raining bits of paper—
a commuter beside me
unfurled his black umbrella—
I noticed the margins were singed.
A gilt-framed photo landed at my feet
and raised a cloud. Was I walking in dust?

I bent and licked my finger
and cleaned the faces—a mother and child
blurred by soot, beaming at me.
Could I leave them?

I had no right to that happiness
and the bronze scallops were searing.
Stamped on the back was the word RUTH.

A voice behind me shouted *hurry*
and another screamed *mercy.*
I braced my shoulders.
All around me were voices
pushing, pushing like men,
and men crying like children,
and a child calling *help*
from behind a pebbled glass door.

The island had been sealed.

2

A policeman said:
*if you breathe that cloud
you will die* as if suggesting
some other escape:

but we did not walk faster
or falter; there was a rhythm
we were obeying, just under the limit
of the weakest in the crowd,
and for years after,
perhaps until the last day,
we would be faithful to it.

The haze united us
and the wrinkles on our faces
became outlined as in greasepaint
in that red dust—

so we left our city, and the cloud settled
on the far shore, and the people there
had no need of names.

Ruth

The face on the flyer
was serene as a god—
below, a phone number
and scratched note:

even if you just glimpsed her,
even if you're not certain.

I bowed to that stare
and flinched at a smudge
where the invisible hand
pressed too hard.

At the curb a rhinestone purse
still held a thimble and a token.

I tripped over two votive candles.
One flame guttered. I knelt
but the wick curled into itself.

That night it rained, you could no longer
smell the steel burning.

When I came back to Union Square
the face was everywhere,
on a red construction cone,

a lamppost, a rental van,
safe in a maze of faces

but the woman had faded—
a cloud with a smudge
where I had seen hair,
the pearl necklace
a string of blobs:

you could still discern
the hand's tremor
but the words had fused
to a solid block:

even if you just glimpsed her,
even if you're not certain.

October Rendezvous

1

We dial a recording
and order vitamin K,
Cipro, twin masks.

Shunted between prompts,
we stare at each other
with deep longing,
drumming our fingers
while the line grows faint.

We borrow a Glock and wrap it
in a chamois cloth and lock
the bullets in a separate drawer—
where to hang the key?

We stockpile Poland Spring
under our bedstead
and feel that bulk
nullify the give
when we make love.

2

Huddled before the news,
we touch the screen—
our bombs rain on Kandahar—
we can't feel them:

just a thrum, the pulse,
a film of dust, a red glow
shining through our nails.

3

We saw it
and can't stop watching:
as if the plane entered the eye
and it was the mind
that began burning
with such a stubborn flame.

We saw the bodies jump
and couldn't break their fall—
now they wait so gracefully
in midair, holding hands.

The Civilian Casualties

1

Wasn't it in the Dark Lord's interest
to keep harping on the civilian casualties?

Didn't it serve him
more efficiently than his own strange weapons—
fire, plague?—didn't it make us guilty?

Winter was coming. There was no plan.
The plan was to keep doing
whatever we did before.

Sometimes instead of bombs
we dropped wheat from a great height—
wheat from our immense stores—
and watched it plummet
in the icy night.

2

Falling objects are so beautiful,
especially when you've grown old
and worry you won't love again—
the word *betray* will intervene
between belly and thigh—

they rotate, that lateral hum
seems a will

stronger than the plunge:
they appear to give off light
though surely it is the full moon
and the great stars with Arabic names:
Aldebaran, Altair:

as the crates shatter
they send up high spires,
pillars, amphitheaters of dust
that the wind inhabits
like a hand in a glove—

then the horizon
closes like a book
and we are flying, rapid and low,
over the friendly desert
that contains parks, rivers,
forests, our parents' house,
the child's red wagon,

and no landing lights,
no wind sock, no white line,
no voice
to guide us safely down.

Searchers

We gave our dogs a button to sniff,
or a tissue, and they bounded off
confident in their training,
in the power of their senses
to re-create the body,

but after eighteen hours in rubble
where even steel was pulverized
they curled on themselves
and stared up at us
and in their soft huge eyes
we saw mirrored the longing for death:

then we had to beg a stranger
to be a victim and crouch
behind a girder, and let the dogs
discover him and tug him
proudly, with suppressed yaps,
back to Command and the rows
of empty triage tables.

But who will hide from us?
Who will keep digging for us
here in the cloud of ashes?

The Reunification Center

We brought pictures of the missing,
held gingerly, by the cropped margins,
as if the eyes were scalding: or food:
steaming casseroles without ladles,
though the night was mild: Evian:
M&M's, which we tried to hand out
in that cordoned-off street
where an ambulance chugged empty:

and each stranger refused, a little pained,
no, no, I'm here to help: we offered aspirin,
stock certificates, a child's rocking horse,
a teddy bear with an empty eye socket,
but no one consented to receive that treasure:

a doctor ashen with fatigue shouted
into a cell phone, shaking it
when it didn't answer, a digger
dozed hugging his shovel,
a survivor, mesmerized by the portraits,
stunned at their beauty, compared them
scar by scar with the faces of the living.

Separation at Burnt Island

A Hike to Little Falls

1

The shell had hardened
and the chick could not hatch
though we sensed its heartbeat
in our cupped hands,
imperious, panicked.

Should we shatter
that delicate casing
scored with faint runes?

Already it smelled of us.
The flock would shun it.

The other eggs glinted,
icy in the toppled nest.

We felt our own pulse
advancing with the same wild purpose
as the heron crossing the river.

2

It was a taint in the rain,
a sweetness in the water,
something else we forgot
to discuss as we climbed here

past Chaux Springs and the Fire Pond,
breathless, exultant, watching
worked land reveal itself,
and above, the false summits,

3

though we packed so carefully:
waterproof matches, compass,
flashlight, freeze-dried rice,

the map carefully sealed
and memorized in two minds.

Germaine River

We took a last sip of Bali Hai
and walked hand in hand
there where the current
is most like the mind.
We let ourselves go

but there was a force
that knew us, struggled for us,
carried us past the shoals,
and deposited us a yard apart
on a spit of quartz sand
under dwarf pine.

There the blank sheen
closed like a book behind us
and the body in reflection
woke, staggered, gasped,
and whispered for us alone
I'm sorry.

Herkimer

At last we had absolute control
over heaven and hell
and 99 percent of God's will
but there was very little we could do
about the lights of Herkimer
flickering in the rearview mirror
like bees logy with pollen.

Had we even been to that town
with its dusty barber pole,
bent speed-limit sign,
fenced-off cemetery,
and bar called He's Not Here

or was it all implied in the name?
We were lovers, soon to marry,
just entering the desert,
in a lopsided argument over justice,
in a bitter fight over mercy,

coming to towns that were just signs:
Lorimer, Winter Wheat, Plumb Line,
and towns that were toppled signs
or signs erased by dust:
Oo . . . E . . . shadow.

If we could label each other,
Good, Bad, Wife, Lover,
we would be safe with the dead
who carry their little tags:

GUILTY . . . SAVED . . .
like lamps across Acheron:

meanwhile those lights
followed us, kindling
instead of fading.
We winced at their reflection
in the dashboard:

had there been a silo?
A little padlocked church?
A brick school
with bas-relief white pillars?

Was there a promise
on a marquee, missing a few vowels?

And we who saw each other
always for the last time—

perhaps we would go down
the long road to childhood
when we finished marriage:

find a gate with one stile
in the center, and enter it:

and we who are these names
glanced at each other
dubiously despite
the careening white line—

in a little tin box
with two cones of light
filling with insect wings,

the pupil of the eye held us,
blacker than the hills
north toward Basalt—

sometimes we leaned over
to undo a button,
pat back a strand of hair,
or whisper a charm—

then we flew
with no mother or father,
no lover, no friend,
into the desert.

North of Althea

We followed Aix River toward the source
three days through box elder.
Often it was just a give under us,
sheen of pollen in the arrow grass,
swerve like the breeze
in runged pine shadow.

This is the test, we thought, shivering
in the sleeping bag, at the center
of a ring of blackened stones,
some split in two.

But we were climbing steadily.
Althea, the Antidolite,
little villages glinting like lures,
at dusk like rubies in a scalepan,
horizontal spark of a windshield
at the edge of the wheat.

We were wearing identical orange hats.
We hated the other for being *I*
whereas we were just a fly's bowstring voice
and the nakedness of kicked stones.

Monotony of the pulse, desire
always too weak or strong,
the voice—clearly not ours—
coaxing us upward.

The river reappeared like a ferret
among flat rocks,
some brutally, elegantly striated
with the hex sign of the horizon.

We passed a shard from hand to hand:
it grew miraculously heavy
and in its bevel we could read
Bronze Age, Mesozoic,
Age of Basalt.

We had come so high
we glimpsed the littoral,
silt ring, and pulsing horizon.
The islands were still possible.

The last night it rained.
We woke tangled, wincing
at the imprint of our nails.
Before dawn a whippoorwill called.
We climbed into the ring of the flashlight.
We stumbled until first light
isolated the crook of a birch.

We knelt at the source
and that water was so bitter
we choked, it was a word on our lips,
marriage—when we left
a sparrow rolled in our spillage,
flinching like us at the cold.

Picnic at Opposite Island

The story captured us
and would not release us
so we thought it really happened—

that we betrayed each other
on that small glove-shaped inlet
ruled by the fine script of sandpipers:

a rabbit watching
from behind a bush
like a child making rabbit ears:

when we rowed back
it was the boat in the story,

the 'lovers,' the 'thwart,'
the 'folded clothes,'
the oarlock 'crying like a child,'

Canada to starboard,
Drummond Rock, hoot of a ferry,
'mid-August,' 'neap tide.'

Then the shorebirds called
with cold estranged voices
not to us, not to us,

to someone so present
she could only be the breeze—
darkness, faint guitar
picking its way from note to note,

the home jetty, a lamp brightening
until all it showed was nakedness.

Cape Ann

We walked just shy of the surf
arguing how we would live
after the ceremony, and once

I stepped on the perfect skull
of a kestrel, seeing it
clearly as I destroyed it:

red algae like maps of itself
crumbled under our bare feet:
we kept coming back

to that wavering foam barrier
(like a fragile swerving horizon
or the line between man and woman)

though we loved to wander
in the suck and glint
of receding breakers

shielded from the other's voice;
we were wounding each other
so we might marry

and sometimes glanced together
complicit at a mothwing sail
luffing to windward.

A trawler hauling seines
vanished over the sea rim,
funnel first, then riprap wake.

So we decided
on the child's two names
and the lighthouse flashed

withheld as a bead of blood—
each step we retraced
rippled with flow tides.

Home

1

You winced in the rocking chair,
waiting for your water to break.
I paced the outer edge
of the raffia carpet.

A radio was playing,
as if there were still news,
traffic, war, sports, weather,
in that huge country before dawn.

But we couldn't break our trance.

Saint Luke was nine miles away.
Sirens peaked and diminished.
We couldn't hear them.

Our blood hammered in time
to the pulse in the other heart.

2

We bundled the newborn
over the doorstep
into the white room
we'd dusted so carefully.

We sat on the bed,
snow on our lapels,
while the child slithered between us
with a swimmer's wriggle.

Then one boiled water, one swept,
one wrapped duct tape
around the cord to the lamp,
one counted pins,
one folded diapers,

in absolute silence,
not even terrified,
as if we were in command,

and after a few days
the invisible snow stopped,
music resumed
behind the paper-thin wall,
traffic roared again,

and always, one held the child,
safe on that journey
away from the body.

War on the Ants

With shoes, with hammers,
with our bare hands, with poison
that sends the cat reeling,
with lenses and mirrors,
by patience and cunning
we have sworn victory
and if it eludes us
what kind of husbands
will we be? Praise God

there is only the one ant
like a traveling comma
and there are thousands of us,
millions, with fabulous weapons,
immense hammers, hands
toughened in brine and pitch,
reflexes honed by prayer,
fasting, and endless practice—

for this moment
when the ant appears
and vanishes
in a single gesture
and the house is secure
and fills with the cries of strangers.

Magnet Bay

1

The tall cedars sway without wind
because there are children
camped at the crests
spying on parents
and when one approaches
they make the cries of birds
but too expertly:

should we coax them down
with honey and cookies
or order them down?

Our mistake: to bargain:
a crow answers, a finch,
a bobwhite, the high hawk
offended but strangely indifferent.

2

How they must love us, to hide
so ruthlessly, then hunt us
among the monsters of the green cave
where the ghost crab with eyes on stalks
perches over his victims' bones.

3

Now it is beginning to rain.
We have the tent spread out
but miss the tarp and the bag
of orange pegs—still it is a marvel
how small our house could fold.

4

The youngest bosses her doll:
Sleep, can't you sleep?
Sleep, little fidget.
Does the wind scare you?

With her thumb she covers
the staring eyes.

I'm tired of being me, she whispers
and I hold her, I offer her
a whelk shell and safe dreams
but she finds the catch.

All you ever do is promise.

The Marriage in Canaan

How the dog loved to chase his ball
even in the rosebushes
where thorns tore his coat.

How there was another life.

That long summer
a bee circled our house
diligently, like a toy airplane.

It happened that the child
unhooked her swing
and carried it away
in the crook of her arm.

Happiness undid us.
We wanted to live on a road
exactly like this
but seen from a distance—
the frisbee in midair by day,
by night the books massed
in their fiery window.

Our gravel driveway
seemed to repel us,
pushing us gently up.

Once the dog found a dead bat
and pawed it gently,
puzzled for a second, then certain

when he rolled the torso over
and saw a cloud of tiny wings.

The child spread thimble cups
on a towel under the elm
and filled them from a broken pot.

Perhaps she was inviting the mind
to sip, one finger raised,
and never thirst again.

Soon it was dusk, she slept
guarded by a little white cloud
in a corner of the mirror.

Night fell like a leaf
and we lovers crept
into those huge names
—wife, husband—

drew them up to our chins
and woke in Mother's house
in Father's orchard.

Then the mockingbird called,
sick with loneliness.

Burnt Island

That island had two villages,
Baker and Chester; two industries,
lobster and watercolor; two churches,
Baptist and Universalist,

an oxidized green Esso pump,
a beauty parlor, a padlocked library
with wind-soft blue shutters
where I left the arc of a fingernail
for my blaze home.

       And in the interior
vast carboniferous forests,
where eohippus eludes hyaenodon
and monarchs a yard wide
are stalked by a famished dragonfly.

The map suggested a mountain
whose peak we never saw,
a system of caves . . .

But when we asked a local
he nodded judiciously
and sketched a journey in dust:
take Chester Road toward Baker,
find the plank across the creek,
take two lefts, no, two Norths . . .

That August we walked endlessly
to exhaust ourselves
so we might rest from each other
for a blink or a heartbeat.

And the child followed
at a fixed distance
kicking a smooth white stone
that veered toward Canada,
mumbling names of burweed,
hiding so well we never knew,
or climbing a scrub oak
to find a thrush egg, an acorn lid,
the tight ring of the ocean.

Origins of Desire

After Lynn Margulis and Dorion Sagan

1 ANIMA

This is the groundwork:
Autopoiesis, constant creation
of the self from sunlight.

But gender varies like the breeze
and sex like tides.

Thousands of quasi-sexual fathers
might fuse and form our body,
just visible on a net-veined leaf.

We might cannibalize each other
and the indigestible rind
become the partner.

Or we might trade
genes for *male* and *female*
like beads or playing cards.

But we are each built of water
locked in a membrane.

The same comet-tail sperm
in starfish, ginkgo, and human.

2 RED GIANTS

Hydrogen caught fire
in the forge of the nebulae
and fused to carbon—

our element, pliant,
ready to combine
with any foreign body:

magnesium, calcium, contaminants
released in the great explosion
that lit the sky like a match

before there was a mind to understand
the advantages of annihilation.

3 ARCHEAN MICROBES

When the dust cloud
rolled back from earth
we died of radiance—
the sun burnt holes
in the inmost braid of DNA.

Light-nourished, light-poisoned,
we migrated into rock
or traded little damaged pieces
of self between each other,

enshrining separation inside us,
creating the blueprint
for an absolute stranger.

4 THE UNLIT ROOM

The mind is a story
that found a way
to tell itself—but who
is the confidant, who
the eavesdropper,
who gropes for a switch
along this invisible wall?

In our narrow bed
we hear the catch
of the other's breath,
faint Muzak, an ice machine,
a late goose honking
toward the idea of south.

Between five and six
we whisper our presentiment—
great herds going blind
in Patagonia, a moth species
extinguished at every breath.

We exaggerate a little.
Those extra zeros
hold our reprieve.

Perhaps it is too late
and we can still make love
and catnap toward dawn.

But even if we close our eyes
we are still married.

Space Marriage

1

Our starship blew up
between Alpha Centaur
and the Second Quadrant
but we could not die
because we had stolen
the god's codes:

so we kept traveling
deeper into the future
just ahead of our bodies
and when we had sex

we felt ourselves scattering:
there in the galactic cold
where the immense numbers
begin to rotate slowly

we put on the robes
of the night sky.

2

An alien had imprisoned me
in that lunar module
that was just the thought

I and he fed me
what *I* would eat
and mated me
with the one *I* loved:

strange ordeal
there in the Second Quadrant
in Spica's radio-shadow
where the gravity of time
pulls dreams from a sleeper's mind:

bitter confinement
naked on a falling stone.

3

We built robots who built robots
that had a little of our hesitation,
our fatigue, our jealousy,
our longing for Alpha, peace, nonbeing . . .

They covered our long retreat,
those machines, that looked
like can openers or outboard motors,
but with the guilty air of husbands
and the god's fixed stare.

4

It was a system:
we loved each other,
the war began on Vega,
we watched the hurtling lights,
and the silence drained us.

5

Out of spit and dust
we made two lovers
who set fire to the world.

The Dark Universe

The universe is growing vaster and darker,
wives are no longer visible,
the little wheels of the can opener
have grown blunt and turn on themselves,
Aldebaran and Vega still blaze in the depths,
but they are just words.

What caused those swiftly receding worlds
to take the shape of the optic nerve?

It was a catch in the numbers
we could not foresee—zero and one
would become life and death

but only to each other
as the mind knows its power
only in darkness, and its undying love
in a quarrel over a lost spoon.

We rented that dim airless cabin
between Chaux Springs and the nine waterfalls
from June to August, to reconcile, and by dint
of halfhearted hide-and-seek
and short journeys in a leaky skiff
we arrived at the last night.

The children played with the flashlight,
making an enormous wheel in the night sky—
who knew there was no give there—

the dark universe was the exact contour
of the guy rope we forgot on Burnt Island;

until slowly that halo let us go;
we unscrewed the tiny bulb
and found an oozing battery.

Cheats, liars, at home on earth,
we slept in each other's arms,
lulled by the faint hiss
of fireflies in the Coleman lamp.

Marriage in a Rented House

The cat felt herself becoming
just like the dog:
she struggled with the urge
to slobber over bones,
fetch sticks, and turn
three times before a dream—

the dog was the opposite,
rarely licked himself, could not purr,
had one life, could not contain himself,
curled always at the feet of the Masters.

How stubbornly we loved each other
though we hated ourselves.

A sparrow sang in a language
translated from the dawn.
A fly walked on you, on me,
as if on the moon.
In her crib the child cried
for mother and father.

Summer of buckling stairs,
roses peeling from the wall,
endless preparations
of a mouse in the plaster.

Our rented house was settling
slowly back into clay,
bits of seashell, spider hairs.

The cat could wait. The dog could not.
We loved each other. In a dream
the child cried: *take me home.*

Separation at Burnt Island

Brothers and sisters, who live after us,
don't be afraid of our loneliness,
our dented wiffle ball, the little kerf
the dog chewed in the orange frisbee.

Don't grieve for our kite; not the frayed string
that clings to your ankle, not the collapsed wing.

We lived on earth, we married, we touched each other
with our hands, with our hair that cannot feel
but that we felt luxuriously, and with promises.

We made these bike tracks in the sand
—don't follow them—and this calcined match head
is the last statue of our King.

We lived between Cygnus and Orion,
resenting the blurriness of the Pleiades,
in a house identical to its neighbors—
stepwise windows, ants never to be repelled,
TV like a window into the mind
that can't stop talking, redwood deck
facing the gulf.

Everything was covered with sand: the seams
of the white lace dress, the child's hinged cup,
the watch (even under the crystal), the legal papers.

We were like you, or tried to be. We divided our treasures
(a marble with no inside, a brooch from Siena),
signed our names with all our strength, and went home
in two directions, while the marriage continued
without us in the whirling voice of gulls.

Defenses
of the Ocean

for Rachel Carson

Diaspore

There is a barrier
that locks me in.
I must endure this sleep
until what seals me off

is burnt, frozen, exposed
to ax blow, erosion, rain,
noon, twilight, starlight:
then I will flower,

everything in me—
triple-folded leaf
of the female organ,
leaf shoot of the male,
whorled together
like petals in bloom—
will be explained
as if by a voice:

now I must pass
unknown to myself
through the belly and gut
of the northbound sparrow.

Nine Crows

We grew old
so we cried out
in cold supercilious voices,
the least surprised
presence on Burnt Island.

We staked claims
in midair, skew to each other—
no common measure
between our unearthly glide
and manic flap.

Sometimes we trembled.
Mostly we waited.
Remember our bright eyes?
Our sarcastic weariness?

To pass time we played tricks.
We pretended to fall from the sky
—*oh no, I've forgotten how to fly*—
or minced outraged
at a spindled leaf.

You found us in the coppice
in latticed light
inert as mittens
and bent to pick us up
but we creaked away
on suddenly huge wings,

rowing six inches
above the broken needles,
pulled off course
by an icy laughter
we could not control,
resurrected from your pity.

We loved to madden the high hawk
with our clumsiness,
until he contracted it
flying hunched, plummeting in spasms,
like a baffled falling stone.

Remember the barren orchard
where you paced at twilight,
counting us until we lured you
to the wrong side of zero?

Once you entered our gaze
your steps became deafening—
consequence, consequence—
your body a system
of pores, dander, spent wind,
so tightwound and loosely spavined
you winced and turned back.

You never saw us eat
but sometimes in matted grass
a thing consumed by us—
a squirrel huddled
in a net of holes.

We perched at the tips
of Coleman's pines
bowing them only slightly
until the night sky
held us like a compass point.

You couldn't tell us apart
although you installed a story
between Cygnus and Orion
and fastened birth and death
on the clouded Pleiades.

At the river wharf
we sifted kelp
strand by strand
—*finished, still to do*—
until we found a snail:
then our eyes brightened:
we would find a way
to enter that white house
no bigger than the eye.

We too felt loved
from an appalling distance—
Sirius or the trembling gap
between Lyra and Vega.

Nothing is left
of the forest on Burnt Island
except your rage
to be known by us.

Fringillidae

finch

Still in the sac
before I am
I hear my mother's song—

fluent, baffled,
two clicks and a long
cascading note.

I do not know
there is an outside
or an opposing will

but I know the cost
of what seems effortless.

Newborn in sleep
I practice that catch:

you the watcher
looking into my mind
with laser and sonoscope
measure the waves
in the dreaming brain:

two brief stumbles
and a long fall.

It is the trance of desire
faint and cold
in the drizzling pines—

a pattern on a gauge
graphed on an axis—

the music that created you.

Six Red Spiders
in the Elm at High Falls

How to describe the web?
It is already in our minds,
already our minds—
how we know ourselves
and imagine knowing ourselves.
As you might dream your universe
no bigger than a fist
at the instant of origin
and ask: *what surrounds it?*
—so the web is our choice.
It shines in midair.
We may walk across it,
immune to its suction
and secreted poisons.
It trembles, like us,
its principle is *give,*
the prey is the center
but when he struggles
he winds himself deeper
sending a message
which reaches us
as we are building the next web—

so days, clouds,
the breeze itself,
are just a voice.

Hymenoptera: The Ants

for Deborah Gordon

1

They say we are descended from the wasps.
Can't you feel it?
Once we had a house in the sky
and swooped with a terrifying drone.

Now we are sentenced to this silence
in which our acts become our language.

We carry the bodies of the dead
into the underground hives
and keep our paths swept.

We walk the wilderness
in broken circles
searching for the seed
that contains tamarack, Burnt Island,
the high crests flashing with evening.

Since we lost the Kingdom
to time alone, we make ourselves
always purer, more obedient
to the will (we have no tablets),
carving our doors and lintels
deeper underground.

2

There is one who is huge,
and stoops, and counts, as if
those zeros were the seed.

To baffle him
we make subtle mistakes—
we entomb a fleck of dung
among the fathers, or wrap mica
in strange paper shrouds
and tend it like pupae.

3

We build a city, and after five years
and many dynasties, unbuild it,
and erase our complicated scents
so the earth smells just of rain.

We send our Queen
on her wobbly flight
with her entourage of suitors—
tiny jawless males
who will never eat in this world—

we who have wings only in death.

4

Our wars are fought in the desert,
without mercy, but somehow sleepily—
perhaps the sun makes us drowsy?

The plan is, we grip the enemy
with our jaws below the waist
and try to saw him in two.
He reciprocates.

Sometimes he dies
of thirst, loneliness, distance from the colony,
and we must return to our duties
with those mandibles gripping us,
without anger, or with the anger of the wind.

This is the whole problem of victory:
the severed parts go on thinking.

5

The fire ants have built an empire
high above us.

We know their generals—
Arcturus, Aldebaran—
and their pupae, the Pleiades.

For a thousand generations
they have planned to invade us
from that golden hive.

And we have built an absolute weapon—
silence—when it is perfect
it will abolish them
and the earth, and the kneeling watcher
whose lips frame such immense numbers.

We have wings in death.

The River Monarchs

Sex was a cold bright mirror
dangled in front of our eyes—
if we came too near

it gripped and transported us
and we never saw our sky again—
just fringes of clouds.

Sex was a blade of timothy
we kept climbing;
it buckled under us.

When we trembled,
when we pirouetted,
sex was the thing we missed.

Were we immortal
longing to be mortal,
or the other way around?

We found a niche in the breeze
but the current had no choice.
Still we walk backwards

on that powerful scrim,
dragging our soaked wings
toward the icy source.

Tardigrades

water bears

We are slow
and the swift stream
fascinates us.

How to explain the riffle
when we grope our way
to the tip of a fern
over several weeks?

Our enemies are fungi
who hunt us mercilessly
in the moss cushion.

But we escape
by sleeping a hundred years
curled up in ourselves.

There is another winter
and when it strikes
we lay frozen eggs—
nothing will hatch
until the world heals.

We confide the blueprint
of our cells to a drop of sugar
and go into a dream,
Cryptobiosis, the hidden life.

Our legs contract,
our brains wither,
our long dorsal heart
shuts down, we turn
inward, inward.

We are the aftermath,
tuns, minute barrels
you may find in creek moss,
in an untended web,
on the smooth side of a pebble,
stain on a stain.

After fire and absolute zero
we emerge, segmented ticks

inching forward entranced
not so much by water
as its tension.

Eel Migration

Memory is the stream:
wave-form the current
glides through, V of ripples
marking a submerged boulder,
algal filaments, cove
no bigger than the body,
rotifers, copepods,
the light broken—

By filtration of starlight,
concentration of salt
in the mind, by degrees of nothing,
we find a way
to the mating-place
where memory is the ocean.

Five Marine Solitudes

THE SAND LUGWORM

We dream of the part of ourselves
that the gull bit away,
so intensely
it grows back.

Everything in the world
is a wing, a claw,
a coat of scales.

We have no defense
except this trance
in which we return to the body
—the shape of the wound—

and fit in our carefully sculpted tunnel,
except for our protruding heads.

Also we give off light.

NOMEUS

The Portuguese man-of-war jelly
is not one *I* but a thousand:
every tentacle, each sac
grew from a different egg
—a colony of selves—

and I, Nomeus,
sliver of a fish,
flit through those poison arms
where my enemies can't catch me.

I survive by luck,
vulnerable as they
to the sting
but not possessed
by the fury of the hunt.

BOAT SHELLS

Locked in our armor
and forged in a chain
slowly we change
from male to female
as the wind shifts
and Burnt Island darkens
from blue to slate.

BARNACLES

If we could rest for a moment
from our grievance
against the racing clouds—

if we could rest from being white—
if we could rest from resting—
if there were a way not to cling—

if there were an exercise
we could practice
so as not to be held
by our intentions—

there would be no shore.

THE WAVE

I ruled this world
until the sea slug
discovered that it suffers.

Brittle Star

1

I feel the soft tug
of the starfish—I know it
by its gentleness—

but it persists
longer than my closing muscle
can keep my clamshell shut.

2

Then that stomach enters
and consumes me: I am the starfish.
Cut off my arm: it grows back.
When my center hardens

3

I am the brittle star
fossilized in basalt
a thousand thousand years ago

before the great nets
began drifting untended

and the nine-mile line of hooks
uncoiled as a sign
that you discovered immortality.

Defenses of the Ocean

HOLOTHURIOIDEA

sea cucumber

When attacked
I extrude my guts
(they regenerate),

the enemy feasts there,
triumphant, disappointed,
and the *I* that contains
the mind of the ancestors
darts sideways:

Carapus, alert little fish,
grows old in my anus,
proud to touch
the horizon with each fin.

BRYOZOA

moss animals

We are the armies
that conquered long ago
and now build our palace—

passive, passive—
where there is current
to lave our excrement.

ACMAEIDAE

limpet

I fasten myself to you
with byssal threads—
suffering, desire—
when you hunt me
I am the searching gesture.

CHAETOGNATH

glass worm

I graze on the barbed hook
and wander through baleen.

Newborn, I was a pinprick.
Now I am transparent.
Green lamps of Mnemiopsis
light my path

and I find smaller things
to feast on: zoeae,
desmids, noctiluca,
winged flagellates.

Each that I rend
was a universe.

Who knew the invisible
had such tireless jaws?

NOTACANTHIDAE

spiny eel

Even my picture in your book
is not me but my cousin
Halosaurida or the shadowfish
Ultimosias mirabilis or the wrasse
also known as the blenny.

I have no backbone. I am no eel.
I can't last a night in captivity.

Tomorrow I swim freely
in the hidden ocean.

RAJIDAE

skate

My single egg is a masterpiece—
horn encased in hide—
when my one pup is strong enough
to break out, she is my double,

experienced in loneliness,
hunger, and the sense
of being surrounded
by a mysterious obstacle.

Other fish, plaice, dace,
release streams of larvae—
even in the throat of the net
they might be immortal—

but I must watch my self leaving me,
a great headless wing
flying dutifully, absentmindedly,
toward the edge, the bottom, the surface.

JANTHINA

violet snail

Confined to the surface
I blow a bubble, then another,
I make a raft of bubbles
and cling to it—if I relax my hold
even a blink, I will drift down
for fifty years, then begin
the long journey into stone.

HALOBATES

water strider

Pensive I walk
in the trough of the wave
like an old scholar
with his hands behind his back
trying to solve a theorem . . .

My home was a footprint in Kansas
glinting with dew
but I began thinking
and here I am

in the open Atlantic
always in the trough
while above me
the crests shatter
and each drop of water
returns in an ellipse
seven feet long
to its starting point:

but always I have found
another foothold,
even in the hurricane
there is an inch of calm,
even the maelstrom
is just an agitation—

The Indian Ocean towers over me,
then the Antarctic.

All I need is solitude
and I will find the answer
to this problem of marriage.

OMMASTREPHES PTEROPUS
squid

I emit a cloud of ink
which looks like me—
the little squiggles
are tentacles—

perhaps you imagine a will
behind that terrifying Image
but I am gone, safe
in the corner of the eye.

When I grow old
and descend to the abyss,
the place of monsters,
cold, dark, no current,

I release a cloud of radiance.

The Pressure Zone

We who live at the bottom
sense the irresistible currents
high above us: Humboldt, Benguela:
precincts of banner kelp and plankton,
and above that, violence
of the surface, shadow
of wings—auk, kittiwake, squa.

Our bodies are flat as veils
under six miles of water.

We hunt in the abyss
with a light we turn off
at will, and the enemy
also has a lamp
to shine or extinguish.

If we drift above our zone
air rushes into our bladders
so strongly we can't resist
and drown upward.

You know us by our eyes,
huge or atrophied.

We grow old at the foot
of these submerged volcanoes
—Pico, Volandia.

Rain from the dead
sustains us, silicate
of a billion decomposed shells,
volutes returning to salt,
mast to cloud, prow to mist,
the only remaining solids—
shark teeth, whale earbones—
spiraling to basalt:

to know this world, watcher,
do I have to conceive it
without you, since I can't
tell you from desire?

There are two possible endings:
darkness and the hostile light.

The Little Sea

1 DNA

Before me, just rain,
lightning, heavy surf.

I came to the shallows
at Ilapse, in the Archeozoic,
liking the odds against me.
A trillion to nil.

Out of carbon, sulfur,
nitrogen, and phosphorus,
I alone found the way to die—

a pact between sunlight
and something small beyond belief.

I knew no predator
except the self.

2 DIATOMS

We reproduce by dividing—
does that surprise you?

Almost all surface,
we soak up gold, copper,
iron, cobalt, and hoard them
behind our minute flanged walls.

We confiscate daylight
and transform it
into a long argument
between you and me
locked in a glass box.

We are brief.
Three generations
before nightfall.

So close to nothing
we are still yoked
to that labor, perfection.

We are the wealth of earth.

Chalky residue
on a feathered oar,
ghost sheen on the otter net—

these are outposts of our empire.

3 THE VANISHING POINT

The paths of foam
appear to converge
at a fixed point
but only in the inner eye,
that tiny whorled chamber
identical in squid and human.

To arrive at the body
is to make landfall

on Burnt Island
in gaff season—reek of dung,
looped shad guts, banked fire.

A willow whips back
but if you take two steps
you come to the horizon

and the world without us.

The Many-Eyed Nemerteans

ribbon worms

The edge of cloud shadow
suspended over combed surf
struggles to become us
because we have the Self
while it has none
and must coax a phase
out of a billion annihilations
and thread that pulse
between polar cells
to infer a charge,
an absence—

Mercury and Saturn
might be our reflection
but they are blind,
sealed in ellipses,
whereas we have multiple eyes
that crawl over our bodies
recording the gradations
of twilight, salt, and gender.

We grow temporary gonads
for the instant of union
and fertilize our eggs
in a gel string.

Our blood is yellow
though we have no heart.
We eat the Annelids
and they us.
Our spines are water
and cannot be broken.

We are branched like leaves
an eighth of an inch long
propelled by Coriolis.

We have no brain and our name
means *infallible.*

Leuresthes Tenuis

grunion

1

We mate, the tide
strands us on Burnt Island
where we can't breathe—daylight
harsh as the mind between dreams.

We cover the egg-mass
side by side, jetsam
in sand, targets.

In a moment, surf
returns us to deep water.

2

Roe glints in the template
our bodies left, quickening
on fast ground, naked
to beak and claw,
hardening in salt air
until the incoming breakers
carry that sac
back to the gulf.

3

So it is just timing, keeping
a certain distance from yourself,
learning to plummet,
to be abandoned,
to use the lull
between two tides—neap

and ebb, dead time
when the blood of the starfish
reverses direction—

and enter the night sky.

Pelagos

for Theodor Schwenk

1

This is the medium:
threshold between gas and solid,
chemically neutral,
transparent.

The wave-form glides before the wind,
a lull imprints the star-grid.

Our law is this trembling,
the hand's hesitation
after long labor.

2

Shatter the surface.
A waterspout gathers
in perfect tension
between sphere and straight line.

If a straw drifts in,
or a sailor's body,
it sails counterclockwise and down
always at the same angle
to Polaris and the point of entry

3

and the whirlpool forms
in the embryo in the womb
and becomes the ear,
the rhythms of the seiche
harden to intestine,
liver, pancreas, sex,
the branching ripples
are the neural network—

4

until that blank sheen heals
from the wound of the oar.

Mysticeti

blue whales

1

I dove to the sea floor
and blew a bubble-net
and the herring were caught,
sealed in mammal-sky,
and delivered where you basked
in the last shaft of evening.

Sometimes I spoke to you
in a code of clicks and whistles,
soft but audible
half a continent away—
not a name, not music,
just conversation, just this language
in which we and the sea are alone.

2

Later we made love
and dozed side by side;
every nine minutes a tremor
drove us to the surface for air—
such was the power
of the mind in darkness.

Cetacea

gray whales

Eyes dim with cataracts,
the elder beached,
nosing too shallow
there where the creek mouth
clogs with nenuphar.

We followed her.
We stranded ourselves
and felt the kelp fronds
pop under our fins

but when the men came
with saws to carve us
(with long poles
to goad us back)

we did not resist
(we refused to escape)—

we could not leave her
alone on that shore
though to stay was death:
not just to us

but to the clouds, the wind,
moonlight, the tide,
the frantic strangers.

The Granite Coast

We are like you
because we scrape these boulders
with sharp coiled tongues
which we unroll progressively
as our mouths wear out:
when you open us
you find the cliff inside us
though we are tiny as an eyelash;

we are like you
because we are born by the billions
and float into the open ocean—
as if we were entering
our own plenitude
which is the certainty of death
and the slim chance of sunlight—
and the ones who never return
are the faint roar
in a sleeper's ear;

we too make little threads
mysteriously in our genitals
to hold us to the ledge,
and in our nests we weave
mica and our victims' bones;

we are kin to you
because the great tides

advance and retreat inside us—
though you may call it salvation
or adaptation, it is a circle
in which the living and the unliving,
the souls and anti-souls,
grow their intricate spiral shells;

We are I, I, I—
there is only one of us
and with our frail tentacles
we build the dawn sky.

We are helpless on this sea
full of thinking knives
and coral shards nibbled
by ravenous flowers.

We wage war on ourselves
and drift through our armor
like cloud shadow.

We graze on each other
and the limbs grow back
secreting dark sugar.

The gull will destroy us
and the plumed worm Amphitrite
make a home in our eyes.

Yet our bodies are shaped
exactly like the resting place,
we fit in each other

like silence in desire,
we live another second
or much less, less than a blink,

until the code comes to know itself
and the mind dreams another mind
that will survive it
there, in the bright curtain of spray.

Notes

Burnt Island is in no way a scientific book. But the second half reflects an outsider's fascination with biological language and the horizons it opens. With no claim to understanding or factual accuracy, I'm enthralled by the worlds of naturalists, oceanographers, and neuroscientists.

I'm deeply indebted to the luminous mind of Rachel Carson, without whose insights I could never have written the third suite. Her books *The Sea Around Us* and *The Edge of the Sea* inform "Eel Migration," "Five Marine Solitudes," "Brittle Star," "The Pressure Zone," "Leuresthes Tenuis," "The Granite Coast," and many other poems.

"Origins of Desire" was inspired by *Origins of Sex: Three Billion Years of Genetic Recombination* by Lynn Margulis and Dorion Sagan, *Early Life: How Cells First Evolved* by Lynn Margulis, and *The Periodic Kingdom* by P. W. Atkins.

"Hymenoptera: The Ants" was written after reading *Ants at Work* by Deborah Gordon.

"Diaspore," "Tardigrades," and "The Many-Eyed Nemerteans" were inspired by *Five Kingdoms: An Illustrated Guide to the Phyla of Life on Earth* by Lynn Margulis and Karlene V. Schwartz.

"Pelagos" was informed by *Sensitive Chaos* by Theodor Schwenk.

"Defenses of the Ocean" owes a debt to information contained in *The Life of the Ocean* by N. J. Berrill, *Abyss* by C. P. Idyll, and *Broadsides from the Other Orders* by Sue Hubbell.

Other books that have been important to me include *Synopsis and Classification of Living Organisms*, edited by Sybil Parker; *The Empty Ocean* by Richard Ellis; *The Evolution of Consciousness* by Robert E. Ornstein; *How Brains Think* by William H. Calvin; and *Consciousness Explained* by Daniel C. Dennett.

Acknowledgments

Some of the poems in this collection have been previously published in the following: "Diaspore" (published under the title "Flying Seed") and "The Reunification Center" in *The Atlantic Monthly;* "My Father's Closet" in *The American Poetry Review;* "Brittle Star" and "North of Althea" in *Areté;* "4 A.M." in *Barrow Street;* "Ruth" in *The Brooklyn Review;* "Origins of Desire" in *The Cortland Review;* "Space Marriage" in *Fence;* "Cape Ann" and "A Puzzle at Saint Luke" in *Field;* "A Walk in Giovanna's Park" in *Heliotrope;* "Home" and "Night Flight" in *The Kenyon Review;* "The Little Sea" in *The Literary Review;* "The Dark Universe," "Defenses of the Ocean," "Fringillidae," "A Hike to Little Falls," "Nine Crows," and "Picnic at Opposite Island" in *The Manhattan Review;* "The Last Judgment" in *The North American Review;* "October Rendezvous" in the *Orlando Sentinel;* "Marriage in a Rented House," "Saint Luke," "Searchers," "Separation at Burnt Island," and "War on the Ants" in *Poetry;* "Cetacea" and "The Pressure Zone" in *Poetry Ireland Review;* "The Civilian Casualties" and "The Evacuation Corridor" in *Poetry London;* "The Ring" in *Poetry Wales;* "Eel Migration," "The Many-Eyed Nemerteans," and "Tardigrades" in *The Saint Ann's Review;* "Germaine River," "Herkimer," and "The Marriage in Canaan" in *TriQuarterly;* "Two Nights in the Men's Shelter" (part 1) in *Willow Springs;* "October Rendezvous" in *Poetry After 9/11: An Anthology of New York Poets,* ed. Dennis Loy Johnson and Valerie Merians (Hoboken, N.J.: Melville House, 2002).

Thanks to the MacDowell Colony for the Leila Wallace Fellowship, to the Corporation of Yaddo for the Howard Moss

Fellowship, and to *Poetry*, for the Frederick Bock Prize, for work in this book.

I'm grateful to Philip Fried, Howard Stein, Hal Sirowitz, Marc Kaminsky, and Anneliese Wagner.

Special thanks to my editor, Deborah Garrison.

A NOTE ON THE TYPE

This book was set in Bodoni, a typeface named after Giambattista Bodoni (1740–1813), the celebrated printer and type designer of Parma. The Bodoni types of today were designed not as faithful reproductions of any one of the Bodoni fonts but rather as a composite, modern version of the Bodoni manner. Bodoni's innovations in type style included a greater degree of contrast in the thick and thin elements of the letters and a sharper and more angular finish of details.

Composed by NK Graphics,
West Chesterfield, New Hampshire
Printed and bound by United Book Press,
Baltimore, Maryland
Designed by Virginia Tan